Israel and the Arab World

Gil Zohar

VOICES FROM
ISRAEL

Mitchell Lane
PUBLISHERS
P.O. Box 196
Hockessin, Delaware 19707

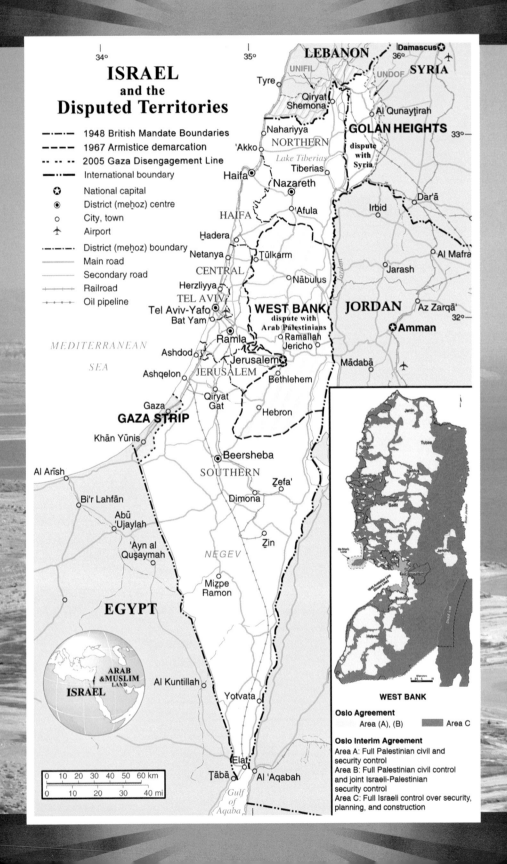

ISRAEL
and the
Disputed Territories

- –·–·– 1948 British Mandate Boundaries
- – – – 1967 Armistice demarcation
- –·· –·· 2005 Gaza Disengagement Line
- –··–··– International boundary
- ✪ National capital
- ◉ District (meḥoz) centre
- ○ City, town
- ✈ Airport
- –·–·– District (meḥoz) boundary
- —— Main road
- —— Secondary road
- +–+–+ Railroad
- +·+·+ Oil pipeline

LEBANON

Damascus ✪

UNIFIL

SYRIA

Tyre

UNDOF

Qiryat Shemona

Al Qunayṭirah

Nahariyya

GOLAN HEIGHTS

NORTHERN

dispute with Syria

'Akko

Lake Tiberias

Haifa

Tiberias

Nazareth

HAIFA

Afula

Irbid

Dar'ā

Ḥadera

Netanya

Tūlkarm

Al Mafra

CENTRAL

Jarash

Herzliyya

Nābulus

TEL AVIV

Tel Aviv-Yafo

WEST BANK

JORDAN

Az Zarqā'

Bat Yam

dispute with Arab Palestinians

32°

Ramla

Ramallah

✪ Amman

Ashdod

Jericho

MEDITERRANEAN

Jerusalem

SEA

Ashqelon

JERUSALEM

Māāba

Gaza

Bethlehem

Qiryat Gat

GAZA STRIP

Hebron

Khān Yūnis

Al Arīsh

Beersheba

SOUTHERN

Ẓefa'

Bi'r Lahfān

Dimona

Abū 'Ujaylah

Ẓin

'Ayn al Quṣaymah

NEGEV

Miẓpe Ramon

EGYPT

ARAB & MUSLIM LAND

ISRAEL

Al Kuntillah

Yotvata

Elat

Tābā

Al 'Aqabah

Gulf of Aqaba

| 0 | 10 | 20 | 30 | 40 | 50 | 60 km |
| 0 | 10 | 20 | 30 | 40 mi |

WEST BANK

Oslo Agreement

Area (A), (B)   Area C

Oslo Interim Agreement
Area A: Full Palestinian civil and security control
Area B: Full Palestinian civil control and joint Israeli-Palestinian security control
Area C: Full Israeli control over security, planning, and construction

Mitchell Lane
PUBLISHERS

Printing   2   3   4   5   6   7   8   9

Library of Congress Cataloging-in-Publication Data
Zohar, Gil, author.
 Israel and the Arab world / by Gil Zohar.
    pages cm
Includes bibliographical references and index.
 Summary: "Israel and the Arab World, written from an Israeli viewpoint, examines Israel's geopolitical position in the Middle East and the Arab world. The status of many Palestinians as stateless people and refugees is often in the news. This book explains how this tragedy was created and is being perpetuated. The narrative examines Zionist chauvinism, Arab rejectionism, the long and convoluted search for peace, and the history of asymmetric warfare and terror. Israel's relationship with Egypt and Jordan-with whom it has peace treaties-is discussed. The reader will meet some Palestinians, including Palestinian Americans, and will encounter a symbol that evokes co-existence and peace. Parallel to the Palestinian-Israeli conflict is a war for public opinion. The author encourages each reader to have an open mind and to avoid stereotypes as they seek to unravel the tangled truth. Peace begins in one's heart, and not from government decrees; certainly not from propaganda. It is the hope in this undertaking that we may all merit to contribute to peace and understanding in the global village which is our planet Earth"—Provided by publisher.
 ISBN 978-1-68020-000-3 (library bound)
1. Arab-Israeli conflict—Influence—Juvenile literature. 2. Israel—Foreign relations—Arab countries—Juvenile literature. 3. Arab countries—Foreign relations—Israel—Juvenile literature. 4. Palestinian Arabs—Juvenile literature. I. Title.
 DS119.76.Z64 2015
 327.5694017'4927—dc23

2015008404

eBook ISBN: 978-1-68020-001-0

ABOUT THE COVER: Jerusalem's Muslim shrine the Dome of the Rock was built more than 13 centuries ago; it also marks the site of Judaism's holy Temple.

PUBLISHER'S NOTE: This book is based on the author's extensive work as a journalist based in Jerusalem, Israel. Documentation is contained on pp. 58–59.

The Internet sites referenced herein were active as of the publication date. Due to the fleeting nature of some web sites, we cannot guarantee they will all be active when you are reading this book.

To reflect current usage, we have chosen to use the secular era designations BCE ("before the common era") and CE ("of the common era") instead of the traditional designations BC ("before Christ") and AD (*anno Domini,* "in the year of the Lord").

PRONUNCIATION NOTE: The author has included pronunciations for many of the Hebrew words in this book. In these pronunciations, the letters "ch" are not pronounced like the "ch" in "children." Instead, the letters "ch" represent the Hebrew letter chet, which sounds like a "kh" or hard "h" sound, similar to the "ch" in "Loch Ness Monster."

PBP/PBP4,34,35

CONTENTS

Introduction

This book is dedicated to my friend Hajj Ibrahim Abu el-Hawa (Ah-bu el-HAH-wah). He brings to life the hospitality of the biblical patriarch Abraham, whose name he bears. Hajj Ibrahim is dedicated to the search for peace in the spirit of Abraham, the father of the Jewish and the Arab people.

Born on Jerusalem's Mount of Olives in 1942, when Palestine was ruled by Britain, Hajj Ibrahim still owns the home where he was born. Yet he is not a citizen of any state he can call his own. Without a passport, he travels the world with an Israeli *laissez-passer* document, promoting understanding among the peoples of the Middle East.

We are friends despite our very different backgrounds. I am Jewish. I work as a tour guide, writer and artist. I was born in Canada, but have been an Israeli citizen for many years. Hajj Ibrahim is Muslim. He is a retired telephone technician. He is stateless.

Conflicts in the Middle East are often in the news. In this book focusing on the story of Israel and her Arab neighbors, I share my personal perspective. This book includes a bit of the history of the country some people call the Holy Land. We also explore the complicated roots of the Palestinian-Israeli conflict, and Israel's relations with two neighboring countries with whom she has peace treaties, Egypt and Jordan. You will meet Palestinian-Americans, and I will share a symbolic story of our quest for peace.

In that spirit, I share a quote from the Quran, (KOR-an), the holy writings of the Muslim faith:

"And we said thereafter to the Children of Israel, 'Dwell securely in the (Promised) Land.'"
—Quran, Sura 17:104

Gil Zohar

Hajj Ibrahim Abu el-Hawa and his wife Naíma

On May 14, 1948, David Ben-Gurion declared Israel's independence in the waning hours of the British Mandate. The ceremony was held at the Tel Aviv Museum of Art, today preserved as Independence Hall. A photo of Theodor Herzl (1860–1904), the founder of the Zionist movement, hangs on the wall behind Ben-Gurion.

CHAPTER 1
The Roots of Conflict

The founding of the modern state of Israel in 1948 was experienced as a dream come true for the Jewish people. It was a return home for a nation that had been **exiled** from its biblical homeland for two thousand years, and suffered terrible persecution leading to the Holocaust. During waves of immigration in the nineteenth and twentieth century, the population of Jews living in what they called the Land of Israel grew rapidly. These immigrants came from across the globe, including Africa, Asia and America, but especially from Eastern Europe.

For the Arabs who lived in the country previously ruled as a mandate of the British government, and before that as part of the Ottoman Turkish Empire, this dream-come-true for the Jewish people was a catastrophe, which also sparked the anger and resistance of the Arab states surrounding Israel.

This book is about the history and the relationships between Israel and its Arab neighbors, both the Arabs who now live in the State of Israel and the two adjoining areas—the West Bank, the cities of which are ruled by the Palestinian Authority, and the Gaza Strip controlled by Hamas, and two neighboring Arab countries.

Today's strife has its roots in the late nineteenth century when growing numbers of Jews began to return to the Land of Israel. They were inspired by Zionism—the political movement to restore the Jewish people to its ancient home. The conflict between those early Zionists and the Arabs who also lived on this sliver of land between the Jordan River and the Mediterranean Sea has persisted for more than a hundred years, and has yet to be resolved.

Viewed from abroad, that conflict between Israel and the people today known as Palestinians, appears to define current events in the region. But for those who live in this area, life goes on. Israel's economic and cultural horizons have expanded dramatically since the country was founded. A population of 600,000 has grown to 8.3 million.[1] Half the world's Jews live in Israel, a democracy with a rich and lively Hebrew culture, and a thriving high-tech economy.

Even as the strife continues, many Israeli wearily shrug their shoulders at what they call "the situation," (ha-matzav, in Hebrew—ha-ma-TZAV). The root of the present long conflict dates back to events and ideas more than a century ago. Nineteenth and twentieth century Hebrew essayists and Zionist thinkers pondered what was to be the connection between the country's existing tradition-bound Arab population and the masses of Jewish immigrants, many keen to build a socialist utopia.

Among those writers was Asher Zvi Hirsch Ginsberg (1856–1927). He is better known by his Hebrew pen name, *Ahad Ha'am* (ah-CHAD ha-'AM) which literally means "one of the nation." His pen name is taken from a biblical phrase.[2] He was born in Kiev, then part of Imperial Russia, and he later lived in Odessa. He visited the remote Ottoman Turkish province known as Palestine as a writer. His strong words foreshadowed the conflict between the Jews who were creating a new society there and the Arabs who tilled the soil and lived on the land for generations.

In his critical report, *Truth from the Land of Israel*, Ahad Ha'am noted: "We tend to believe abroad that Palestine is nowadays almost completely deserted, an uncultivated wilderness, and anyone can come there and buy as much land as his heart desires. But in reality this is not the case. Anywhere in this country, it is difficult to find Arab land which lies fallow. . . ."

"But when the day will come in which the life of our people in the Land of Israel will develop to such a degree that they will push aside the local population by little or by much, then it will not easily give up its place."[3]

Ahad Ha'am's warning was not heeded in his lifetime. His concerns were brushed aside by most of his contemporaries, Zionist pioneers who believed that the benefits of economic development in the region would lead the Arabs to put aside their antipathy to another people settling in their midst.

A spiritual perspective was expressed by Rabbi Avraham Isaac Kook (1865–1935), who became Palestine's first Chief Rabbi. In 1908, he wrote with messianic expectation: "The brotherly love of Esau and Jacob, of Isaac and Ishmael, will rise above all the disturbances . . . and transform them to universal light and compassion."[4]

While Jewish immigration and land purchases resulted in some conflict, the lion's share of responsibility for bringing the simmering tensions to a boil belongs to the European powers that dominated the Middle East during and after World War I (1914–1918).

In 1916, French bureaucrat François Georges-Picot (Fran-SOI jhorsh PEE-coh) and his British counterpart, Sir Mark Sykes, reached a secret agreement on the partition of the Ottoman Empire. In an unrelated initiative that took place the same year, the British High Commissioner in Egypt, Sir Henry McMahon, issued a series of letters to the Sharif of Mecca, Hussein bin 'Ali (HUS-sane bin Ah-lee). McMahon promised the Sharif independence if the Arab tribesmen under his influence joined the guerilla uprising against Turkey. That revolt was led by British Colonel T.E. Lawrence, better known as Lawrence of Arabia.

One year later, in 1917, Britain issued the Balfour Declaration, which promised to establish a Jewish homeland in Palestine. The promises the British made to the Jewish residents of Palestine and the Jewish diaspora were clearly in contradiction to the commitments it made to the leaders of the Arab world. The British also trampled the tentative 1919 agreement reached by Sharif Hussein's son Prince (Emir) Faisal, pronounced FI-sal, and Chaim Weizmann (Chai-EEM WEIZ-mann), the Russian born, British chemistry professor and leader of the Zionist movement. Prince Faisal and Weizmann held friendly talks aimed at establishing a Jewish state in Palestine with its capital in Jerusalem,

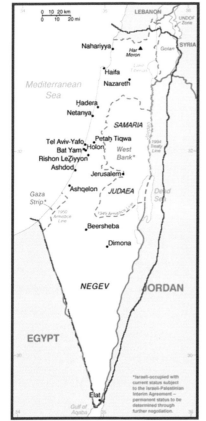

Chaim Weizmann (left) with Prince Faisal wearing Arab headdress as a sign of friendship. Today it would be unthinkable for an Israeli leader to wear a kaffiyeh.

Map showing boundaries (in red) of the proposed protectorate of Palestine, as suggested by the Zionist representatives at the 1919 Paris Peace Conference, superimposed on modern boundaries.

Emir Faisal's party at Versailles, during the Paris Peace Conference of 1919. Left to right: Rustum Haidar, Nuri as-Said, Prince Faisal (front), Captain Pisani (rear), Lawrence, Faisal's slave (name unknown), Captain Hassan Khadri.

and a united Arab kingdom, including the Arabian Peninsula with its capital in Damascus.

Britain and France overrode that possibility, together with the newly established League of Nations. The two countries joined forces to divide the 700-year old Ottoman Empire that collapsed in 1918 at the end of World War I. Britain and France cut up the former empire into quasi-colonial mandates with boundaries that did not take into account the ethnic and religious divisions in the region. The mandates they created also did not give adequate attention to the way scarce water resources would be used. This set the stage for a century of conflict in the Middle East continuing to the present.

The new boundaries were agreed upon at a post-World War I gathering, the San Remo Conference, held in 1920 in Italy. The Arabs protested against the resolutions, calling it *an-Nakba* (Arabic for "the disaster"). Rioting broke out in Palestine, Syria, and Iraq. In Palestine, those riots, which were called disturbances, continued in 1921 and 1929, and led to the Arab Revolt of 1936–1939.

The Arab Revolt included a general strike, the withholding of taxes, sabotage, the assassination of British officials, and the murder of Jewish and Arab civilians. The violence was a protest

Jews evacuate the Old City of Jerusalem after Arab riots in 1936. In the face of repeated violent protests, Britain steadily backpedalled on its commitment to create a Jewish homeland in Palestine.

Britain used severe measures to suppress the 1936-1939 Arab Revolt in Mandate Palestine. Here soldiers of the Coldstream Guards are seen evicting Arab rebels from Jerusalem in 1938.

against the growing number of Jews making their way to Palestine, as well as anger about worsening economic conditions and other factors.

Although some Jews called for the creation of a bi-national state in Palestine, most understood that the harsh reality did not offer room for dialogue. It seemed apparent that the Jews would have to hold strong until a future generation of Arab leaders would accept Israel as part of the modern or perhaps post-modern Middle East.

This strategy was best expressed by the Russian-born Zionist leader, Ze'ev Jabotinsky (Zha-boh-TIN-skee) (1880–1940). In his 1923 essay, *The Iron Wall (We and the Arabs)*, he wrote:

"Zionist colonization must either stop, or else proceed regardless of the native population. Which means that it can proceed and develop only under the protection of a power that is independent of the native population—behind an iron wall, which the native population cannot breach."

He argued that the Jews must first establish a strong Jewish state. He believed this show of strength would eventually lead the Arabs to "drop their extremist leaders, whose watchword is 'Never!' and pass the leadership to the moderate groups, who will approach us with a proposal that we should both agree to mutual concessions."[5]

This Iron Wall viewpoint was widely held among leaders in the years of pre-State Israel, when the Jewish community of Palestine was known as the *Yishuv* (Hebrew for settlement, pronounced yi-SHUV). The belief that the Jewish State endures by virtue of its military strength and nuclear arsenal remains until this day. Many Israelis believe that peace negotiations will not bear fruit until the Palestinian leadership stops thinking that the Jewish state is illegitimate, and gives up its hope that Israel will ultimately collapse.

Does that perspective reflect the way Palestinians view the State of Israel in the twenty-first century? To gain insight into the situation today, it is helpful to understand the different circumstances of those who call themselves Palestinians.

- One and a half million Arabs, self-identified as Palestinians, are citizens of Israel.
- A quarter of a million Palestinians live in Jerusalem and have Israeli identity cards, which entitle them to varied government benefits, although they are not citizens of Israel.

- 4.5 million Palestinians (2.7 million in the West Bank and 1.8 million in the Gaza Strip) have a measure of self-rule under the Palestinian Authority (West Bank) and Hamas (Gaza Strip)
- Five million Palestinians live in exile scattered across the Arab world, Europe, the United States and Canada.[6]

For the 1.5 million Palestinians who are citizens of Israel, the issues of personal and political identity are complex. Despite difficult periods of conflict, Jews and Arabs live side by side in relative coexistence in a number of Israeli cities, including Jaffa, Haifa and Acre. In Jerusalem, terror and politics take a greater toll.

Relations between Israelis and West Bank and Gaza Palestinians have evolved over the years, but today are severely limited. After the Six-Day War in 1967, there was a period of relatively friendly interaction between Israelis and Palestinians in the newly captured territories.

From 1967 until the 1990s, tens of thousands of Palestinians from the West Bank and the Gaza Strip worked in Israel, primarily in agriculture and construction. Many learned Hebrew and developed relations with their Israeli employers. Some admired Israel's democracy and even saw it as a model for the independent Palestinian state they hoped to create.

During those years, many Israelis visited the West Bank and Gaza. Commercial ties developed as Israelis shopped, ate at local restaurants and had their cars repaired by local mechanics. There were even Israelis and Palestinians who went into business together.

Those tenuous and unequal relations were shattered with the outbreak of the 1987 intifada (in-ti-FAH-dah). Intifada is an Arabic word for popular uprising, whose literal definition is

Arab children participate in a local demonstration in the Muslim quarter of Old Jerusalem in August 2014 to call attention to the difficulties of the Palestinians living in Gaza.

"shaking off." It was sparked by false claims of Palestinians killed by Israelis, which led to local demonstrations, rock-throwing, blocked roads, and tire burnings. The violence grew into ongoing attacks with hand grenades, Molotov cocktails, and guns that continued through 1993.

A second revolt, known as the Second Intifada, began in 2000 and continued with suicide bombings and terror attacks through 2005. The flashpoint was the visit by then Prime Minister Ariel Sharon to the Temple Mount in Jerusalem, viewed by the Arab world as a purposeful attempt by Israel to disrupt the Muslim presence on the Haram ash-Sharif holy site.

Israeli riot police try to quell clashes that erupted outside the al-Aqsa mosque in Jerusalem's Old City in September 2000, following a visit to the Haram ash-Sharif holy site by Israeli Prime Minister Ariel Sharon—an event that sparked the outbreak of the Second Intifada.

In October 2000, thirteen Israeli Arabs were killed by Israeli police during the course of a week of rioting. Despite a commission of the Israeli Supreme Court to investigate, the rioting and the deaths led to a crisis that has not been fully resolved in the uneasy relations between the State of Israel and its Arab citizens. Mutual hostility and anti-Arab sentiment are rampant.

In response to the waves of violence during the course of the Second Intifada, the government of Israel began to build a separation wall. This barrier cut off much of the West Bank from Israel along the 1949 armistice line, known as the "Green Line." But it also incorporated some Palestinian land near Israeli settlements built after 1967.

Since the wall went up, West Bank and Gaza Palestinians have needed special permission to visit Israel. They are not allowed to use Ben-Gurion Airport, for example, but must travel to Amman or Cairo. The separation of populations is mutual: Israel also forbids its citizens to enter Palestinian cities such as Bethlehem, Ramallah and Jericho. In 2005, Israel unilaterally withdrew from the Gaza Strip, uprooting 8,500 Israeli Jews who had built a network of settlements and farming communities there known as Gush Katif.

The Palestinian response to Israel includes an international campaign encouraging businesses and countries throughout the world to adopt boycott, divestment, and sanctions (BDS) against the Jewish state. Although the BDS campaign has not caused serious economic damage to Israel, it does harm the country's image by appeals to international cultural and intellectual figures to boycott the Jewish state.

Today Israelis and Palestinians, and their leaders, remain deadlocked. Both sides criticize and dehumanize the other. Both claim the moral high ground, and view themselves as taking defensive actions to protect themselves against a cruel enemy.

THE BALFOUR DECLARATION

The Balfour Declaration was written by British Foreign Secretary Lord Arthur James Balfour and sent to Lord Lionel Rothschild, a leader of the Jewish community in Britain. Dated November 2, 1917, this simple one-page note marked a turning point in the history of Zionism. For the first time, a world power was giving official support for the establishment of a Jewish homeland in Palestine. The full text of the Declaration, below, was included in the mandate given to Great Britain at the 1920 San Remo Conference:

His Majesty's government view with favour the establishment in Palestine of a national home for the Jewish people, and will use their best endeavours to facilitate the achievement of this object, it being clearly understood that nothing shall be done which may prejudice the civil and religious rights of existing non-Jewish communities in Palestine, or the rights and political status enjoyed by Jews in any other country.[7]

Lord Arthur James Balfour

Some 700,000 Arabs fled or were deported from the villages and cities of Palestine in 1948 during the first Arab-Israeli war.

WAR REFUGEES—The Plight of the Palestinian People

British rule in Palestine, mandated by the League of Nations and based on the Balfour Declaration, lasted from 1917 to 1948. During those three tumultuous decades, Zionist Jews who had immigrated to what was known as Mandate Palestine proudly called themselves Palestinians. Many of the business and cultural ventures they founded bore the country's name. The English-language daily newspaper established by Zionists in Jerusalem in 1932 was called *The Palestine Post*. Only in 1950 was the newspaper renamed *The Jerusalem Post*. At the time, Arabs living in Palestine did not identify themselves with the name Palestine. Their culture and language linked them with greater Syria, an area including Syria, Jordan, and Lebanon.

In 1947, the General Assembly of the newly-established United Nations passed a resolution to partition Palestine into separate and independent Arab and Jewish states. The Arab leaders in Palestine and the Arab countries surrounding the former British mandate rejected the resolution, and launched a war against the Jews of Palestine. For the brand-new country that called itself Israel, it was the War of Independence. However, for the Arabs who lived in Palestine, it was a disaster. They called it the *Nakba*, the very same term that Arabs had used to describe to the European division of the Arab territories of the Middle East in 1920.

During the 1948 War, the Kingdom of Jordan annexed the territory it called the West Bank. This region is also known by its biblical name, Judea and Samaria. The Jordanians also seized the eastern half of Jerusalem, dividing the city with barbed wire and minefields the same ways that postwar Berlin was divided.

Egypt, which also joined the war against the establishment of a Jewish State, captured a swath of land along the Mediterranean coast around the city of Gaza which became known as the Gaza Strip.

Thus Egypt and Jordan prevented the Arabs of Palestine from declaring their own state.

Some 711,000 Arabs fled or were driven from their homes in the course of this war. Under the auspices of the United Nations Relief and Works Agency for Palestine Refugees in the Near East (UNRWA), the displaced people were housed in refugee camps established in the West Bank and Gaza in historic Palestine, and in the neighboring countries of Lebanon, Syria, and the Emirate of Transjordan. (In 1948, Emir Abdullah I renamed his country the Hashemite Kingdom of Jordan.)

The 1967 Six-Day War between Israel and its Arab neighbors led to a second wave of refugees. The number is estimated to be between 280,000 and 325,000. About half of those people had also been refugees of the 1948 war, which led to Israel's independence. In Arabic, this second exodus is called *an-Naksa* (the setback, pronounced an-NAK-sah).

As an outcome of these wars, the homes and villages of these refugees mostly no longer exist. The people either fled or were driven out during the wars. Those refugees—and their children and grandchildren—still identify themselves as displaced Palestinians. They insist on their right to return and rebuild their lives in the lands that have not been in their hands for many decades. In Arabic, the term for the "right of return" is *haq al-Awda* (hak al-AW-dah).

Palestinian refugees demand the right to return to their ancestral villages and homes. Called Haq al-Awda, that right of return is symbolized by the keys to the houses people fled in 1948. Today most of those houses no longer exist. Seen here is the entrance of the Aida Refugee Camp—one of three in the West Bank city of Bethlehem.

Where do those refugees now live? UNRWA began assisting Palestinian refugees in Gaza, the West Bank, Jordan, Syria and Lebanon in 1950. Nearly 70 years after the partition of Mandatory Palestine, UNRWA continues to operate a network of schools, hospitals and clinics. The tent cities of the refugees have turned into neighborhoods with concrete buildings supplied with water, electricity, satellite dishes and the amenities of modern life.

Even after the creation of the Palestinian Authority in 1994, UNRWA institutions have continued to exist. They operate alongside institutions that were created by the Palestinian Authority—and not in their stead. In UNRWA-supported refugee camps in other Arab countries, the Palestinians are denied passports by their host countries. Their status as stateless refugees receiving humanitarian assistance remains frozen.

What will be their future? The terms of a possible peace settlement between Israel and the Palestinians have yet to be determined. Israel is prepared to negotiate the return of some refugees and their descendants, and to offer restitution for lost property. But the question of the settling of the refugees remains a stumbling block in negotiations that have been stop-and-start for more than two decades. Other issues proving equally difficult to resolve are the borders between a future Palestinian State and Israel, and the status of Jerusalem and its holy sites.

THE DEBATE OVER THE ROOT CAUSES
OF THE REFUGEE PROBLEM

Palestinians blame Israel for the estimated 711,000 refugees created as an outcome of the 1948 war (which actually took place from 1947–1949).[1] Israelis claim that the Palestinians left in response to orders from their own leaders, or as a consequence of the war waged by the Arab states against what became the State of Israel.

Meron Benvenisti, (Ben-ven-IS-tee), who has served as Deputy Mayor of Jerusalem, shared his perspective in a book called *Sacred Landscape: The Buried History of the Holy Land Since 1948*. He acknowledges the many detailed studies that support or refute the claims of both sides. He points out that the preoccupation with this question does not address whether the leaders of the Arab people had the power, or the will, to halt the mass flight. He points out that the Palestinian leaders' greatest failing was that they abandoned their people and ran away to safety in Beirut, Cairo or London. In Benvenisti's words, "They had left them like sheep without a shepherd, and that disgrace could not be eradicated by laying all the blame on others."[2]

As described in this chapter, an estimated 711,000 Palestinians fled or were displaced and some 400 Arab villages were destroyed. Approximately 100,000 Arabs remained in the territory that became the State of Israel, and became citizens of the new state. Some 40,000 of those Arab Israelis were not permitted to return to their original homes and had to settle elsewhere. They did not receive compensation for the lands they fled, or were driven from, during the war. In 1950, Israel passed the Absentee Property Law, by which abandoned land reverted to the State of Israel. For the Palestinians, this is a great injustice that has never been rectified.[3]

From the Israeli perspective, the territory came into the State's hands as an outcome of a war started by its Arab neighbors. That war threatened the very existence of the Jews who lived in what was then Palestine. Israel also points to the larger number of Jews (between 800,000 to 1,000,000) who were forced to flee their homes in the Middle East and North Africa. The vast majority of those refugees settled in Israel. They were never compensated by the Arab governments who seized their land and property.[4]

Palestinian Arab leader Hajj Amin al-Husseini brought disaster upon his people with his uncompromising attitude toward Britain and the Jews. During World War II he lived in Berlin, and aided Nazi Germany. Here he is seen with Bosnian Muslim Waffen-SS volunteers whom he recruited. Those soldiers perpetrated atrocities during the Holocaust.

CHAPTER 3
UNCLE AND NEPHEW—
The Bloody Legacy of Two Palestinian Leaders

A range of leaders, from militants known for their acts of terrorism to professors known for their learned books, have made the case for the Palestinian people on the world stage. In this chapter, I will focus on two well-known figures of the twentieth century: the Muslim religious leader Hajj Amin al-Husseini, (al-Hus-SANE-ee), and his nephew Yasir Arafat, (AH-RAH-fat).

From my perspective, they bring to life words that said by Israel's past foreign minister and diplomat Abba Eban (1915-2002), who described the Palestinians as "never missing an opportunity to miss an opportunity."

Yasir Arafat's uncle, Hajj Amin al-Husseini, was the Muslim leader who held the religious title of Mufti of Jerusalem. (He was born about 1897 and died in 1974). He was not ashamed to openly declare: "There is no place in Palestine for two races. The Jews left Palestine 2,000 years ago. Let them go to other parts of the world where there are wide vacant spaces."[1]

During the 1920s and 1930s, al-Husseini's henchmen murdered members of rival clans who did not join him in his fierce opposition to Jewish immigration to Palestine and to British rule in the region. After Britain decided to arrest the Mufti for his violent opposition to their rule, he fled to Nazi Germany and settled in Berlin. During World War II, al-Husseini used his influence as a well-known Muslim leader to recruit

Muslims from Bosnia to serve in Nazi Germany's army. Those soldiers carried out horrific war crimes.

Al-Husseini escaped trial at the Nuremburg War Crimes Tribunal following World War II, and returned to the Middle East. He rejected the 1947 UN partition plan for Palestine that had been approved by the international community. Instead, he vowed to drive the Jews into the sea, to complete the slaughter the Nazis had started.

In 1964, al-Husseini's nephew, Yasir Arafat (1929–2004), founded the Palestinian Liberation Organization. For more than three decades, the PLO refused to seek compromise with Israel, and instead mounted a campaign of terror aimed at destroying Israel. Other Palestinian terrorist groups took inspiration from the PLO, including one known as Black September. Black September is known for murdering 11 Israeli athletes at the 1972 Olympics Games held in Munich, Germany.

In 2000, Yasir Arafat rejected the prospect of peace in discussions held at Camp David in the United States, in talks with then-President Bill Clinton and then-Prime Minister Ehud Barak (EY-hud BAH-rak). Clinton and Barak hoped to negotiate a comprehensive settlement of the Israeli-Palestinian conflict, in keeping with the agreements signed in 1993, known as the Oslo Accords. Rejecting agreement, the Palestinians launched a wave of violence and suicide bombings. That terror led to Israel's decision to build what became known as the Separation Fence.

Historian Ephraim Karsh, (Ef-RYE-im Karsh), is especially critical of Arafat. He wrote, "With the exception of Hajj Amin al-Husseini, Yasir Arafat did more than any other person in modern Middle East history to retard the development of Palestinian civil society and the attainment of Palestinian statehood."[2]

According to Karsh, al-Husseini could have chosen to lead his people to peace and reconciliation with their Jewish neighbors, as he promised the British officials who appointed him to his high rank in 1921. Karsh believes that in that case, the Palestinians would have gained an independent state that would have given them much of what was then mandatory Palestine. He notes they would have been spared the flight from the lands where they had lived and decades of exile.

Karsh wrote that Arafat also had the choice of seeking a path of peace, but instead he made the PLO into "one of the most murderous terrorist organizations in modern times."[3]

Karsh believes that it could have been possible to establish a Palestinian state in the late 1960s or the early 1970s. He notes the missed opportunity in 1979, when Egypt signed a peace treaty with Israel. From Karsh's perspective, the Camp David Summit of July 2000 could have turned out differently, too.

Yasir Arafat was succeeded by Mahmoud Abbas (born in 1935), also known as Abu Mazen. Abbas has been chair of the PLO since November 2004 and President of the Palestinian Authority since January 2005. He too has not been able to reach a compromise with Israel. In 2007, he lost control of the Gaza Strip—which Israel had withdrawn from in 2005—to the Islamic fundamentalist group Hamas. Thus, today the Palestinians have two quasi-independent governments which are rivals—one in the Gaza Strip under Hamas, and the other in the West Bank under the Palestinian Authority.

Hamas' rule over the Gaza Strip has included frequent rocket attacks on Israel, which led to three mini-wars with the Israel Defense Forces in 2008–2009, 2012, and 2014. Hamas and Abbas' Palestinian Authority remain locked in a deadly struggle. It is difficult to predict a path that could lead to peace.

Egyptian President Anwar Sadat and Israeli Prime Minister Menachem Begin acknowledge applause during a Joint Session of Congress in which President Jimmy Carter announced the outcome of the Camp David Accords.

CHAPTER 4

ISRAEL'S NEIGHBOR EGYPT—35 Years of a "Cold Peace"

On March 26, 1979, then Israeli Prime Minister Menachem Begin (Men-ah-CHEM Bey-GIN), and President of Egypt Anwar Sadat (AN-war SAH-dat), signed a peace treaty on the lawn of the White House in Washington, DC. The two leaders were awarded the Nobel Prize for reaching an agreement that was the first of its kind between Israel and an Arab country. Tragically, two years later Sadat was assassinated in Cairo by Muslim extremists who opposed his vision of peace.

Egyptian-Israeli relations resulting from the historic 1979 peace treaty can be described as a "cold peace," that is, a peace that did not lead to great cooperation or conciliation between Egypt and Israel. The agreement has however survived the revolutions which have wracked Egypt in recent years. In 2011 President Hosni Mubarak (HOS-nee Mu-BAR-ack), was toppled after 30 years in office. He was followed, for a brief period, by Mohamed Morsi (MOR-see), and then replaced by President Abdel Fattah Sisi (ABD-el FAT-tah See-see).

Today Egypt and Israel have found common cause in their shared battle against radical Islam. It is a consequence of a logic well known in the Middle East: "The enemy of my enemy is my friend." Egypt once exported natural gas to Israel, and now Israel exports fuel to Egypt. Egypt has also taken military action in blowing up tunnels in the Gaza Strip built by militants to smuggle weapons and carry out terrorist attacks on Israelis and Egyptians.

Despite the mutual interests of recent times, few Egyptians visit Israel. In fact, Egypt discourages its citizens from traveling to Israel and from developing economic, cultural and social ties. Similarly, Israel is concerned about poor migrant workers flooding into the country, and makes it difficult and expensive for Egyptians to gain an entry visa to Israel. The Kerem Shalom border crossing near Gaza has been closed for decades, adding many hours to a bus trip from Tel Aviv to Cairo.

Israeli vacationers once enjoyed beach holidays in Egypt's Sinai Peninsula (which was in Israel's possession from 1967 until it was handed over to Egypt in 1982 as part of the Camp David peace treaty). Today, Israel's Ministry of Foreign Affairs issues frequent warnings about the security dangers of such border crossings. Few Israelis visit Egypt, and those who do prefer using a second passport, if they have one in their possession, because they fear possible harm if they are identified as Israeli.

While Egypt and Israel are not at war, there are few encounters between the people of these neighboring countries in real life. *The Band's Visit*, a movie made in 2007, gives a clue to the possibility of how people could discover each other's humanity. The film was written by Israeli screenwriter Eran Kolirin, who also directed the comedy.[1] The film never addresses the bloodshed of the Middle East. Instead, it focuses on the unlikely story of an Egyptian military band that loses its way in a remote Israeli desert town, and the encounter between the Egyptian band members and the residents of the small town of Israelis who get to know them. The film won eight Ophir Prizes awarded by the Israeli Film Academy. When it was first released, though, it was banned in Egypt.

Signs of a thaw in relations between Egypt and Israel are rare. In 2008, the same year the movie *The Band's Visit* was released, the hope of a promising moment was dashed.

Mohamad Sayyed Tantawi (Mu-HAM-ad SAY-yad Tan-TAW-ee), the Grand Imam of Cairo's al-Azhar mosque and Egypt's highest ranking cleric, shook hands with then Israeli President Shimon Peres at a United Nations conference in New York. In Egypt, students burned the Israeli flag and chanted "No to normalization!"

In Israel, there are few public expressions of hostility toward Egypt, though the Israeli attitude toward its southern neighbor is cold and guarded. The well-known Israeli political commentator Eitan Haber expressed it most clearly: "The Egyptians don't like us," he said, "and—why deny it?—we don't like them."[1]

Taba is the only crossing point between Israel and Egypt. The Sinai border is marked by a fence designed to keep out infiltrators and smugglers. Relatively few Israelis and Egyptians visit each other's country.

Once "the best of enemies," Israel and Jordan have been the best of friends since formalizing a peace treaty on October 26, 1994. Today, the two countries share a variety of common interests including cooperation on security issues, the desalinization of Red Sea water, and the allocation of fresh water from Lake Kinneret. Seen here balloons are released into the air during the Israel-Jordan Peace Treaty signing ceremony.

CHAPTER 5
ISRAEL AND JORDAN— The Odd Couple of the Middle East

In 1994, Jordan followed Egypt to become the second Arab country to sign a peace agreement with Israel. The treaty was signed on October 26, 1994, in a ceremony held in the Jordan Rift Valley, near the Israeli border. (The valley is called the Arabah in Arabic, and the Arava in Hebrew, suggesting how close Arabic and Hebrew are.) Israel's Prime Minister Yitzhak Rabin and Jordan's King Hussein shook hands. US President Bill Clinton was present and was accompanied by then Secretary of State Warren Christopher. The ceremony concluded with the release of thousands of colorful balloons.

Egypt welcomed the agreement, while Syria ignored it. However, the Lebanese Shi'ite militia group Hezbollah signaled its unhappiness by launching mortar attacks against towns in Israel's northern Galilee 20 minutes before the ceremony began.

In a region of much conflict, Israel and Jordan have managed to maintain their unusual partnership. Despite many ups and downs, the two countries remain strategic allies. Israel and Jordan share their longest border with one another, and they also share security interests. Jordan stands between Israel and radical Islamic groups to the east and north. Both Israel and Jordan share borders with Syria, a country being destroyed by a four-year civil war and home to the growing threat of the Islamic State.

Jordan supports a two-state solution for Israeli-Palestinian conflict. Historically, Jordan has had uneasy relations with the

Palestinian Liberation Organization led today by Mahmoud Abbas. Jordan also gives Palestinian refugees citizenship, meaning the majority of the 6.5 million Jordanians are actually Palestinians.

It is likely that Jordan is concerned about being blamed by both sides if it were to take on a greater role in Israeli-Palestinian talks.

Yet, even without playing a major role in those negotiations, Jordan remains a key strategic ally for Israel. Writers and analysts of the Middle East note that the importance of Jordan is often overlooked because it's a small state, it does not have oil, and it is not actively at war. But Jordan is deeply affected by everything that goes on in the region. From Israel's perspective, it is a very important state, and perhaps that is not given enough recognition.

The peace treaty was the starting point for Israeli-Jordanian cooperation in a number of areas, including the scarce resource of water. The two countries have consistently worked together on water allocation since 1994. In December 2013, Israel and Jordan signed an historic agreement under which Israel will provide Jordan's capital Amman with 8-13 billion gallons of fresh water from Lake Kinneret each year. Jordan in turn made a commitment to deliver the same amount of desalinated water pumped from the Gulf of Aqaba, (Ah-KAB-ah), to Israel's Negev Desert.

The peace agreement between Israel and Jordan also opened the door to tourism. Many Israelis were eager to visit Petra, one of the world's most famous archaeological sites. Petra was the capital of the ancient Nabateans and a crossroads for caravans conveying the spices of the ancient world. The ruined city is carved out of red sandstone, and surrounded by granite mountains.

In the early days of the State of Israel, young Israeli adventurers would sneak across the frontier to see the wonders of Petra. In fact, in the 1950s, 12 Israelis were shot when they stole across the Jordanian border to view the ancient ruins. Israeli poet Haim Hefer wrote a poem, "The Red Rock," that was set to music to honor their memory.

The number of Israeli tourists who visit Jordan is far larger than the number of Jordanians who visit Israel, yet Jordanian tourism to Israel is on the rise. The number of Jordanian tourists entering Israel has nearly doubled since 2009, with over 80,000 Jordanians visiting Israel between 2009–2014. Today, Jordanians work in the hotels and resorts of Eilat across the border from Aqaba.[1]

Al-Khazneh (the Treasury) is one of thousands of elaborate tombs carved into the sandstone at Jordan's ruined city of Petra.

Salim and Arabiya Shawamreh stand among the ruins of their house in the village of Anata near Jerusalem, which was demolished for the sixth time by Israeli authorities in November 2012. Israel is charged with restrictive zoning regulations and building permits as a way to control the Palestinian population.

CHAPTER 6
PALESTINIANS IN JERUSALEM—Property and the Destruction of Homes

The story of Salim and Arabiya Shawamreh (Sha-WAM-reh), and their seven children bring to life the very difficult realities faced by many of the 250,000 Arabs who live in Jerusalem. Israeli zoning laws make it difficult for Palestinians to get a permit to build a home for their families. If they do build or expand their homes, then their homes may be destroyed because they are deemed illegal.

The Shawamreh family lives in a bungalow in the neighborhood of Anata, a locale that was home to the biblical prophet Jeremiah, some 2,600 years ago. In 2014, the family faced having its property bulldozed—for the seventh time.

After rulings on the matter were dragged out for more than two years, the Israeli Supreme Court rejected the Shawamreh family's appeal not to demolish their home. Yet, no date has been given for Israel's Civil Administration to carry out the court order. Demolition orders are usually carried out by armed police, who break down the front door, remove the contents of the home, and then flatten the building.

The reasoning behind the zoning and building laws are political, and not an issue of urban planning, according to Amir Cheshin, who was the Mayor of Jerusalem's advisor on Arab Affairs and helped form the policy after the 1967 Six-Day War, when East Jerusalem came into Israel's hands. The aim was to make Jerusalem a united city.[1]

Every Friday, Israelis and Palestinians protest the evictions of Palestinians from their homes in the Jerusalem neighborhood of Sheikh Jarrah.

Cheshin points out that Israel's leaders wanted to create Jewish neighborhoods in the newly recaptured regions of East Jerusalem while making it difficult for the Arab population to build. In that way, it was hoped the Arabs would make their homes elsewhere. The discriminatory policy purposely did not take into account the needs—and the rights—of the Arab residents of East Jerusalem.

SETTLEMENTS IN THE DISPUTED TERRITORIES OF THE WEST BANK

Since 1967 when Israel conquered the area it calls Judea and Samaria—and which Jordan and the rest of the world calls the West Bank—the area has been disputed. (See the map on page 2 to view the disputed areas.) For some, it is liberated; for others it is occupied. Today, some 450,000 Israelis live in 121 government-approved towns and cities clustered in various locations across the West Bank. There are also scores of illegal, unauthorized settlements, many on strategic hilltops, where the settlers are squatting on state land with the winking assistance of the government. There is not an exact count of these wildcat settlements.

More than 100,000 Israelis live in Jerusalem neighborhoods and suburbs built on lands that were captured in the 1967 Six-Day War. It may seem confusing that these neighborhoods are located to the north, east, and south of what was called East Jerusalem from 1948 to 1967. (Since 1967, there has been a single merged municipality.)

Israel has a history of dismantling settlements for political objectives—of trading land for peace. All 18 towns in the Sinai Peninsula were removed by 1982 to fulfill the 1979 peace treaty with Egypt. All 21 settlements in the Gaza Strip and four in the West Bank were unilaterally abandoned in 2005.

The future of the Jewish settlements is an issue to be determined in final status talks between the government of Israel and the Palestinian Authority. The great majority of settlers could remain in their homes under a land swap of some 4 percent of the West Bank.

But why shouldn't Jews live in the State of Palestine, just as Arabs live in the State of Israel? Peace and normalization means working and living together, side by side.

A sign forbidding Israelis entry into Area A of West Bank

THE STORY OF A FAMILY LIVING ON JERUSALEM'S MOUNT OF OLIVES

Many organizations protest the difficulties Palestinians face in obtaining building permits. These groups include the Israel Committee Against House Demolitions, Bimkom—Planners for Planning Rights, and Rabbis for Human Rights. According to the Israel Committee Against House Demolitions, more than 2,000 Palestinian homes have been demolished in East Jerusalem since 1967.

One of these cases involves Hajj Ibrahim Abu el-Hawa, who is 72 years old and a well-known member of the Jerusalem Peacemakers, which seeks to promote understanding between people of different religions through the values that their beliefs and cultures share in common.[2] I have dedicated this book to Hajj Ibrahim and share his family's struggle here.

This case may be considered special for a number of reasons. As I mentioned in the introduction, Hajj Ibrahim is not a refugee but a stateless person who still owns the house in which he was born and raised. He is retired after many years of working as a technician for Israel's telephone company. He has an Israeli identity card but no passport or citizenship.

The plot of land Hajj Ibrahim inherited has belonged to his family for hundreds of years. He says that his clan traces its roots back to the Islamic conquest of the Middle East fourteen centuries ago.

In 1995, Hajj Ibrahim paid for and received a building permit for a large home that would serve two generations of his family. He recalls the permit was expensive, and he immediately began the work of digging and building his home, on a steep hillside looking out over the Judean Desert.

The building project advanced in stops and starts, depending on when he had money. In 2000, Hajj Ibrahim's son Umar moved into one unit on the ground floor. Five years later his brother Muhammad moved into another apartment on the same floor. And later that year, a third son moved into the floor above. Each of his sons is married and has children. Two work as taxi drivers, and the third is a plumber.

Hajj Ibrahim decided to add two more floors atop the building for his expanding family, but that addition was not legal, since it had not been included in the original permit. A city inspector took note that the construction did not have a license. The addition was appraised, and its value was determined to be quite expensive. The case was taken to municipal court, and Hajj Ibrahim was convicted of building without the required permit.

Although the judge agreed to a reduced fine, it is still unaffordable for Hajj Ibrahim and his children. Hajj Ibrahim is in frail health and walks with difficulty. His health has been made even worse due to the stress he is suffering because of the threat of the destruction of his home.

Hajj Ibrahim is struck by the injustice of his situation: "Why don't I have the right to build a home for my children?" He feels he is not receiving the respect he deserves as an honorable working man. Though friends and followers in the peace movement have raised some money, Hajj Ibrahim still cannot pay the fine. The court could rule that the illegal addition to his home must be destroyed. In a worst case scenario, he could be forced to pay for the demolition of his own home.

Hajj Ibrahim in front of his house

بيــرة طيبــة

TAYBEH BEER

Daoud and Nadim Khoury pose with a keg of beer at their brewery in Taybeh, 20 miles (32 kilometers) north of Jerusalem. Returning in 1994 from Massachusetts to their ancestral village, the brothers established the only brewery in the West Bank. Their suds have won international acclaim, and Taybeh Beer is today exported to Europe and Japan. But Islam prohibits drinking alcohol—and Muslims constitute some 97 percent of the population of the West Bank. The cultural disinclination against consuming alcohol and Israel's tight control of the West Bank are only two of the Khoury brother's multiple headaches.

A Boston Clan Brings Its Own Beer to Palestine

Daoud and Nadim Khoury (KHOO-ree) are the most well-known residents of Taybeh (TIE-bah), a small village northeast of Jerusalem. The Christian town is linked by legend to the life of Jesus. Since the late nineteenth century, many of its residents have left the village to live overseas. Although Palestinians tend to focus on the refugees of the Arab-Israeli wars, emigration has been part of the history of the region for a long time. Christian families of Taybeh left their homes to find a better life abroad in the Americas, in countries from the United States to Chile and Guatemala.

In the aftermath of the 1993 Oslo Accords, the village gained autonomy under the Palestinian Authority. Today Taybeh has some 2,300 residents, while some 12,000 former residents live overseas. There is a United Taybeh American Association in the United States, and its members keep their ties to their ancestral home. Today, it is estimated that 50 percent of the residents of Taybeh hold US passports.

Daoud (whose English name would be David) and his brother Nadim were born in Taybeh, respectively in 1959 and 1956. They immigrated with their family to Boston, Massachusetts in 1979.

Their father, Canaan David Khoury always dreamed of returning to his village and hoped that it would one day be part of an independent country. Canaan David Khoury was born in Taybeh in 1926, when it was part of the British Mandate of Palestine, and died in the United States in 2002. His two sons decided to leave Boston and resettle in their father's village in the Palestinian Authority.

Nadim means "drinking companion" in Arabic. Nadim studied business administration and when he was a student, he began to brew beer, inspired by American suds like Samuel Adams. He established the first micro-brewery in the Palestinian Authority, and named it after the town where he was born. Taybeh means "delicious" or "good" in Arabic.

The family-run Taybeh Brewing Company makes beers in golden, amber, light and dark varieties, as well as a non-alcoholic version for Muslims, for whom alcohol is forbidden by religious law. The company has won praise and earned awards. The Khourys produce 600,000 liters (about 158,000 gallons) of beer a year. Sixty percent is sold to Palestinians, 30 percent to

Nadim Khoury pours an ice cold Taybeh beer. His family-owned brewery faces difficulties both because of Israeli commercial restrictions and opposition from Palestinian Muslims who oppose the drinking of alcohol.

Israelis, and 10 percent is exported to Europe and Japan. The company hopes to sell its beer in the United States.

The business faces serious challenges, the Khoury brothers explain: Israel limits the water supply to the brewery and also prohibits the drilling of wells. Barriers posed by Israel also make it difficult for them to expand their exports.

Another source of friction are jealous neighbors and intolerant religious extremists. Daoud Khoury, who was mayor (mukhtar in Arabic) of his village from 2005 to 2013, instituted an annual Taybeh Oktoberfest in 2005. But in 2013, the newly elected Taybeh city council refused him a permit; and the festival was forced to relocate to a luxury hotel in the nearby city of Ramallah.[1] That year, someone shot Nadim Khoury (although he escaped serious injury) and his car was torched by a Molotov cocktail. With the rise of Islamic extremism in the Palestinian Authority, Taybeh's town fathers refused to tolerate a festival where men and women mingle together, and people consume alcohol in public.

The West Bank separation wall in Ramallah showing graffiti of Yasir Arafat

The Separation Fence snakes across some 430 miles (700 kilometers) of the West Bank, cutting off most Palestinians from entering Israel. The background photo shows graffiti of Palestinian leader Yasir Arafat (left) and Marwan Barghouti. The latter is imprisoned by Israel, but there are those who believe he may become the leader of Palestine who makes peace.

CHAPTER 8
Israeli and Palestinian Cartoon Characters Symbolize the Dream of Peace

A winding road built during the period of Jordanian rule from 1948 to 1967 leads from mountainous Jerusalem down to the Dead Sea—the lowest point on the face of the Earth. Following the road, you pass a number of Arab towns and then reach a dead-end in the form of an ugly and imposing wall, called the Separation Fence (*Geder ha-Hafrada* in Hebrew). In Arabic, it is known as the *jidar al-fasl al-'unsuri* (the Apartheid wall).

This physical barrier separates the Israeli and Palestinian populations. It was Israel's response to terrorist attacks and suicide bombings by Palestinians who managed to make their way into Israeli cities and towns from the West Bank. Israelis note that between 2000 and 2003, there were 73 such attacks by terrorists, but even after the Separation Fence was partially completed, by the end of 2006, the number of attacks had been reduced to 12. Those who oppose the barrier claim that it is being used to annex Palestinian land under the guise of security. Over the years, there have been many protests and court challenges to the Separation Fence and its route. The Separation Fence has yet to be completed, but its length will be approximately 430 miles (700 kilometers). Over the years, it has become the site of varied activities, from spray-painted art by international graffiti artists to a silent prayer offered by Pope Francis when he stopped along the route of the fence near Bethlehem.

In this final chapter of my book, I will share a personal story that brings to life my dream of the day when the Separation Fence will be removed and Israelis and Palestinians will live together.

I recently made my way to Abu Dis with my friend Hajj Ibrahim Abu el-Hawa, my daughter Bareket, and fellow artist Eva Feld to make our mark on the Separation Fence. We share the belief that a picture is worth a thousand words. Using the universal tools of the graffiti artist—an exacto knife, cardboard and spray paint—we created an image bringing together two cartoon characters, one well known to Israelis and the other famous among Palestinians.

In the image we spray-painted on the Separation Fence, the Palestinian cartoon character, "Handala," (Han-DAH-lah) holds hands with the Israeli cartoon character, "Srulik" (SROO-lick). Few Israelis are familiar with Handala, and likewise, Srulik is not known among Palestinians. We felt that by drawing them together, holding hands, on the Separation Fence, we could illustrate the need to know one another as part of moving forward to true peace.

Handala was created by Naji al-'Ali (NAH-ji al-AL-ley), a well-known Palestinian political cartoonist. In 1948, when he was ten years old, al-'Ali and his family fled their home in the Galilee village of ash-Shajara during the course of what Arabs call the Naqba (the Disaster) and Israelis call the War of Independence. The family made its way to the 'Ain al-Hilweh refugee camp in Lebanon. Over the course of his career, al-'Ali drew more than 40,000 cartoons that harshly criticized Arab leaders and Israel, and lamented the stateless status of his people.

Among his drawings was an image he created called Handala—a barefoot, faceless refugee child. That cartoon character represented his own experience and became a

Handala (right) holds hands with the Israeli cartoon character Srulik.

powerful symbol of the struggle of the Palestinian people for independence and self-determination.

Al-'Ali wrote: "Handala is my signature. I gave birth to this child in the [Persian] Gulf. He was born 10 years old, and he will always be 10. At that age, I left my homeland, and when he returns, Handala will still be 10, and then he will start growing up. The laws of nature do not apply to him. He is unique. Things will become normal again when the homeland returns."[1]

Tragically al-'Ali was assassinated in London in 1987 by the orders of Yasir Arafat—who didn't appreciate the cartoonist's acid humor. But al-'Ali's cartoon image remains alive on the

A Palestinian boy stands next to a cut-out of a Handala cartoon on a hillside in al-Walaja, in the West Bank. The suburb on the next hill, called Gilo, is one of the post-1967 neighborhoods Israel has built ringing Jerusalem to keep the city from being divided again—as it was from 1948 to 1967. Palestinians view Gilo as an illegal settlement.

web, in the press and on T-shirts, key chains and souvenirs found in marketplaces in Jerusalem, the West Bank and the Gaza Strip.

Just as Handala tells the story of the Palestinian people, there is a cartoon character who represents the people of Israel. He is known as Srulik—a nickname for Israel, a common biblical Hebrew name that was also chosen as the name for the Jewish State. Srulik was first drawn in 1956 by the cartoonist Kariel Gardosh (Gar-DOSH), better known by his pen name, Dosh. Kariel Gardosh, or Dosh, was born in Hungary, survived forced labor camps and lost family members to the Holocaust before moving to Israel. He created his cartoon character Srulik as a symbol of his new country, and for decades Srulik faithfully appeared in the daily newspaper Ma'ariv.

Dosh generally drew Srulik as a young man wearing a typical Israeli sunhat and khaki shorts and sandals. Srulik was portrayed as a farmer, who, when called upon, put on his army uniform to serve in the Israel Defense Force reserves. Dosh's editor at Ma'ariv, Shalom Rosenfeld, wrote that Srulik became "a symbol of the Land of Israel—beautiful, lively, innocent . . . and having a little chutzpah."

Spray-painting Handala and Srulik holding hands on the Separation Fence, my friend Hajj Ibrahim Abu el-Hawa, my daughter Bareket, and fellow artist Eva Feld wish to express our hope that the Israeli and Palestinian people may begin to understand one another, and that this understanding will lead to peace. When that is achieved, perhaps the image of Handala and Srulik holding hands will become a symbol for coexistence.

Our dream is that these two beloved cartoon characters, both created by artists who knew persecution and exile, can help bridge the deep gaps between Jews and Arabs in our scarred Promised Land.

CHAPTER NOTES

Chapter 1: The Roots of the Conflict

1. The World Factbook. https://www.cia.gov/library/publications/the-world-factbook/geos/print/country/countrypdf_is.pdf

2. Genesis 26:10

3. Shlomo Avineri, *The Making of Modern Zionism: The Intellectual Origins of the Jewish State.* New York: Basic Books, 1981, p. 123.

4. *The Essential Writings of Abraham Isaac Kook*, Letters 1:112. Jerusalem: Ben Yehuda Press, 2006, p. 142.

5. Jabotinsky Institute of Israel. http://www.jabotinsky.org/multimedia/upl_doc/doc_191207_49117.pdf

6. Palestine Central Bureau of Statistics. http://pcbs.gov.ps/site/lang__en/881/default.aspx#Population

7. The Jewish Virtual Library. http://www.jewishvirtuallibrary.org/jsource/History/baltoc.html

Chapter 2: War Refugees: The Plight of the Palestinian People

1. Wikipedia. Estimates of the Palestinian Refugee Flight of 1948. http://en.wikipedia.org/wiki/Estimates_of_the_Palestinian_Refugee_flight_of_1948

2. Meron Benvenisti, *Sacred Landscape: The Buried History of the Holy Land Since 1948.* Oakland, CA: University of California Press, 2002, p. 124.

3. Wikipedia. Israeli Land and Property Laws. http://en.wikipedia.org/wiki/Israeli_land_and_property_laws

4. The Jewish Virtual Library. http://www.jewishvirtuallibrary.org/jsource/talking/jew_refugees.html

Chapter 3: Uncle and Nephew: The Bloody Legacy of Two Palestinian Leaders

1. The Christian Post. http://www.christianpost.com/news/who-is-responsible-for-the-suffering-of-the-palestinians-117776/

2. Karsh, Efraim. *Palestine Betrayed.*New Haven, CT: Yale University Press, 2010, p. 1.

3. Ibid, p. 252.

CHAPTER NOTES

Chapter 4: Israel's Neighbor Egypt: 35 Years of a "Cold Peace"

1. *The Band's Visit*, http://en.wikipedia.org/wiki/The_Band%27s_Visit

Chapter 5: Israel and Jordan: The Odd Couple of the Middle East

1. YNet News. http://www.ynetnews.com/articles/0,7340,L-4592358,00.html

2. U.S. News and World Report.http://www.usnews.com/news/articles/2014/11/14/israel-and-jordan-the-middle-easts-odd-couple

Chapter 6: Palestinians in Jerusalem: Property Rights and the Destruction of Homes

1. Amir Cheshin, *Separate and Unequal: The Inside Story of Israeli Rule in East Jerusalem.* Cambridge: Harvard University Press, 1999, pp. 31–32.

2. The Jerusalem Post. http://www.jpost.com/In-Jerusalem/Features/Shattered-dreams, April 19, 2012.

Chapter 7: A Boston Clan Brings its Own Beer to Palestine

1. *The Guardian*, http://www.theguardian.com/world/2013/oct/04/palestinian-taybeh-beer-festival-ramallah

Chapter 8: Israeli and Palestinian Cartoon Characters Symbolize the Dream of Peace

1. Common Ground News Service. http://www.commongroundnews.org/article.php?id=28858&lan=en&sp=0

WORKS CONSULTED

Abunimah, Ali. *One Country: A Bold Proposal to End the Israeli-Palestinian Impasse*. New York: Henry Holt, 2006.

Ajami, Fouad. *Dream Palace of the Arabs: A Generation's Odyssey*. New York: Vintage, 1998.

Avineri, Shlomo. *The Making of Modern Zionism: The Intellectual Origins of the Jewish State*. New York: Basic Books, 1981.

Benvenisti, Meron. *Sacred Landscape: The Buried History of the Holy Land Since 1948*. Oakland, CA: University of California Press, 2002.

Berman, Paul. *The Flight of the Intellectuals*. New York: Melville House, 2010.

Binsley, Jack. *Palestine Police Service*. London: Minerva, 1996

Cheshin, Amir. *Separate and Unequal: The Inside Story of Israeli Rule in East Jerusalem*. Cambridge, MA: Harvard University Press, 1999.

Cohen, Hillel. *Army of Shadows: Palestinian Collaboration with Zionism, 1917–1948*. Oakland, CA: University of California Press, 2009.

Gorenberg, Gershom. *The Accidental Empire: Israel and the Birth of the Settlements, 1967–1977*. New York: Henry Holt, 2006.

Halwani, Raja and Kapitan, Tomis. *The Israeli-Palestinian Conflict: Philosophical Essays on Self-Determination, Terrorism, and the One-State Solution*. New York: Palgrave MacMillan, 2008.

Karsh, Efraim. *Palestine Betrayed*. New Haven, Rhode Island: Yale University Press, 2010.

Khalidi, Rashid. *The Iron Cage: The Story of the Palestinian Struggle for Statehood*. Boston, MA: Beacon Press, 2006.

Khalidi, Walid. *Before Their Diaspora: A Photographic History of the Palestinians 1876–1948*. Beirut: Institute for Palestine Studies, 1991.

Kolinsky, Martin. *Law, Order, and Riots in Mandatory Palestine, 1928–35*. London: St. Martin's Press, 1993

Kook, Abraham Isaac. *The Essential Writings of Abraham Isaac Kook*, translation Ben Zion Bokser. Jerusalem: Ben Yehuda Press, 2006.

Krämer, Gurun. *A History of Palestine: From the Ottoman Conquest to the Founding of the State of Israel*. Translated by Graham Harman and Gudrun Krämer. Princeton and Oxford: Princeton University Press, 2008.

Lewis, Bernard. *The Crisis of Islam: Holy War and Unholy Terror*. New York: Random House, 2004.

Mirsky, Yehudah. *Rav Kook: Mystic in a Time of Revolution*. New Haven, Rhode Island: Yale University Press, 2013.

Robinson, Shira. *Citizen Strangers: Palestinians and the Birth of Israel's Liberal Settler State*. Redwood City, CA: Stanford University Press, 2013.

Pappé, Ilan. *The Forgotten Palestinians: A History of the Palestinians in Israel*. New Haven, Rhode Island: Yale University Press, 2011

WORKS CONSULTED

Said, Edward. *The Edward Said Reader*. New York: Vintage, 2000.

Shlaim, Avi. *The Iron Wall: Israel and the Arab World*. London: Penguin Press, 2000.

FURTHER READING

Bickerton, Ian. *The Arab-Israeli Conflict: A History*. London, Reaktion Books, 2009

Ellis, Deborah. *Three Wishes: Palestinian and Israeli Children Speak*. Scarborough, Ontario, Canada (Groundwood Books), 2006.

Sacco, Joe. *Palestine*. Seattle: Fantagraphics Books, 2001

ON THE INTERNET

Al-Awda, the Palestine Right to Return Coalition
  http://Al-Awda.org
American Federation of Ramallah, Palestine
  http://www.afrp.org/
CIA World Factbook
  https://www.cia.gov/library/publications/the-world-factbook/geos/
  print/country/countrypdf_is.pdf
Jabotinsky Institute in Israel
  http://www.jabotinsky.org
Jewish Virtual Library
  http://www.jewishvirtuallibrary.org
Palestinian Central Bureau of Statistics
  http://pcbs.gov.ps
The Electronic Intifada
  http://electronicintifada.net/
United Taybeh American Association
  http://taybeh.org/index.html
Zionism and Israel Information Center
  http://www.zionism-israel.com/

GLOSSARY

Apartheid Wall—part wall and part fence, the Separation Fence (*Geder ha-Hafrada* in Hebrew) and the *jidar al-fasl al-'unsuri* (the Apartheid Wall) in Arabic is a barrier that Israel began building in 2000 in response to Palestinian terror attacks. The obstacle separates the West Bank from Israel, but includes many Israeli settlements located in the West Bank near the wall.

Arabah Valley—a section of the Syro-African Rift Valley, the AravaValley, as it is known in Hebrew, stretches from the south end of the Dead Sea to the Gulf of Eilat. Called in Arabic Wadi Arabah.

Armistice line—the ceasefire line between Israel and Jordan, also called the Green Line, which ended the 1947–1949 Israeli-Arab war. The line marking the territory called the West Bank of the Jordan River is not an international border.

Balfour Declaration—a letter dated November 2, 1917 from Britain's Foreign Secretary Arthur James Balfour to Baron Rothschild (Walter Rothschild, 2nd Baron Rothschild), a leader of the British Jewish community, for transmission to the Zionist Federation of Great Britain and Ireland in which the British government confirmed its support for the establishment in Palestine of a homeland for the Jewish people.

Boycott, Divestment and Sanctions movement (BDS)—the is a global campaign to bring economic and political pressure on Israel to end its occupation of the West Bank captured in 1967.

bi-national state—the bi-national solution, also called the one-state solution, aims to resolve the Israeli-Palestinian conflict by creating a single state in Israel, the West Bank and the Gaza Strip. The claim is that it will offer citizenship and equal rights in the combined entity for all inhabitants of all three territories, without regard to ethnicity or religion.

Bosnia—Today Bosnia and Herzegovina is an independent country in the Balkans. Part of the Ottoman Empire until 1878, Bosnia has a large minority of Muslims, as well as Eastern Orthodox and Roman Catholic Christians. These groups have fought frequent wars in the 20th century.

bureaucrat—a government employee, one who establishes and implements policy

concessions—the softening of a country's policies during negotiations, sometimes involving trading land for peace

desalinization—to remove salt from sea water; In 2005, Israel opened its first major sea-water desalination plant in Ashkelon, using reverse osmosis technology to produce drinking water from the Mediterranean Sea. Since then, four more large-scale desalination plants have come online providing half the country's freshwater supply.

Emir Abdullah—the founder of Transjordan and subsequently king of Jordan, 1991–1951. Assassinated in Jerusalem by a member of the Husseini clan.

Emir Faisal—Founder of the short-lived Kingdom of Syria at the end of World War I, became king of Iraq. Born 1885 and died 1933.

GLOSSARY

exile—expulsion from one's native land by authoritative decree.

Gush Katif—a bloc of 21 Israeli settlements in the Gaza Strip established after the 1967 Six-Day War. In 2005, the Israel Defense Force forcibly removed the bloc's 8,600 residents and demolished it as part of Israel's unilateral disengagement from the Gaza Strip.

Haim Hefer—songwriter and poet Haim Hefer (1926–2012) authored "The Red Rock" about the ruined Nabatean city of Petra. The song was banned on Israeli radio in the 1950s after Israeli adventurers were shot trying to illegally cross into Jordan to visit the site.

Hajj Amin al-Husseini—Haj Mohammed Effendi Amin el-Husseini (c. 1897–1974) was a Palestinian Arab nationalist and Muslim leader in Mandate Palestine. He spent 1941-1945 in Berlin aiding Nazi Germany and raised 100,000 Bosnian Muslim troops. Among his titles was Mufti of Jerusalem, the city's leading Muslim cleric.

Hezbollah—Hezbollah, literally "Party of Allah" or "Party of God" is a Shi'ite Islamic group based in Lebanon.

high-tech economy—Israel today has a high-tech economy, symbolized by Israeli innovations in technology and partnerships with international firms. The country has been dubbed "Start-up nation."

Holocaust—the murder of six million Jews by Nazi Germany and countries that collaborated with Germany between 1933 and 1945.

Kerem Shalom border crossing—near Gaza has been closed for decades.

laissez-passer—French for "let pass," a laissez-passer is a travel document which offers the bearer fewer rights than a passport.

Lawrence of Arabia—British Colonel T. E. Lawrence (1888–1933), better known as Lawrence of Arabia, led the Arab Revolt against the Ottoman Empire during World War I.

Mahmoud Abbas—the President of the Palestinian Authority since the death of its founding leader Yasir Arafat in 2004. Elected for a four-year term, Abbas is in the tenth year of his rule at the time of this writing.

mandate—a system of quasi-colonial states created by the League of Nations following World War I to administer the Middle East territories of the defunct Ottoman Empire. These included French mandates in Lebanon and Syria, and British mandates in Palestine and Iraq.

Mufti of Jerusalem—see Hajj Amin al-Husseini.

Nazi Germany—the racist dictatorship that ruled Germany from 1933 to 1945, led by Adolf Hitler, who instigated World War II and the Holocaust.

Nuremburg War Crimes Tribunal—the trial of Nazi war criminals in Nuremberg, Germany following World War II.

Oktoberfest—a fall celebration of beer drinking and music, originally in Munich, Germany, which has been copied in various other countries.

Oslo Accords 1993—an initial agreement between Israel and the Palestine Liberation Organization whereby Israel would withdraw from areas in the West Bank in order to create a two-state solution to Israeli-Palestinian conflict.

GLOSSARY

Ottoman Empire—the Turkish Muslim Empire, with its capital in Constantinople (today named Istanbul) which ruled much of the Middle East and North Africa until 1918.

Palestinian Authority—the quasi-independent government formed by the PLO to administer the areas Israel withdrew from following the 1993 Oslo Accord.

Palestine Liberation Organization (PLO)—founded in Cairo in 1964, with the purpose of destroying Israel and replacing it with an Arab state.

Quran—Islam's holy scriptures, revealed by the Angel Gabriel to the Prophet Muhammad.

San Remo Conference—the San Remo conference was an international meeting of the post-World War I Allies, held in San Remo, Italy in April 1920 at which Britain was awarded a mandate to administer Palestine based on the 1917 Balfour Declaration.

Sharif Hussein—Hussein bin Ali (1854–1931) was the sharif or "noble" protector of Islam's shrines in Mecca. In 1916 he led a revolt against the Ottoman Turkish Empire.

Sinai Peninsula—the Sinai is a triangular desert peninsula in Egypt about 60,000 kilometers2 (23,000 square miles) in area. It is situated between the Mediterranean Sea to the north, the Gulf of Suez to the west, and the Gulf of Eilat/Aqaba to the east. Israel occupied Sinai from 1967 to 1982, withdrawing in accordance with the terms of the Israel-Egypt peace treaty of 1979.

Six-Day War—June 5–10, 1967, is Israel's greatest military triumph. As an outcome of this triumph, Israel occupies East Jerusalem, the West Bank of Jordan, Egypt's Gaza Strip and Sinai Peninsula, and Syria's Golan Heights.

Taba border crossing—Taba, located 5 kilometers/3 miles south of Eilat, is Israel's only land border crossing to Egypt.

Temple Mount—Mount Moriah is the hill in Jerusalem's Old City that was the site of King Solomon's Temple and King Herod's Second Temple destroyed by the Romans. Since the Muslims arrived in 638 CE, the hill is known as al-Haram ash-Sharif (the Noble Sanctuary) marking the place where Muhammad ascended to the Seventh Heaven.

unilateral—one-sided rather than mutual

Yasir Arafat—Mohammed Yasser Abdel Rahman Abdel Raouf Arafat al-Qudwa, popularly known as Yasir Arafat (1929–2004), founded the Palestine Liberation Organization in 1964. Under the 1993 Oslo Accords, Israel and the PLO began a peace process. But Arafat never completed the transition from terrorist/guerilla fighter to statesman. The cause of his death has remained a subject of dispute.

Zionism—the political movement to re-establish the Jewish state in the Jewish people's biblical homeland. The first Zionist Congress was held in Basel, Switzerland, in 1897 leading to the establishment of the State of Israel in 1948. Today Zionism means building Israel as a Jewish state and increasing aliyah (immigration of Jews to Israel).

INDEX

About the Author

Gil Zohar was born in Toronto, Canada, and moved to Jerusalem in 1982. He is a journalist writing for *The Jerusalem Post*, *Segula* magazine, and other publications. He is also a professional tour guide who likes to weave together the Holy Land's multiple narratives. Gil wrote one hundred pages of *Fodor's Guide to Israel* (7th edition, 2009) and has written tourism promotion material for Israel's Ministry of Tourism. He can be reached at GilZohar@rogers.com or +011 972 (0)524 817 482. For more information see www.GilZohar.ca.

Gil at Yasser Arafat's Tomb in Ramallah